We Can Help!

Carmel Reilly
Mal Chambers

AF584162

Rubbish, rubbish, rubbish!
There is rubbish everywhere!

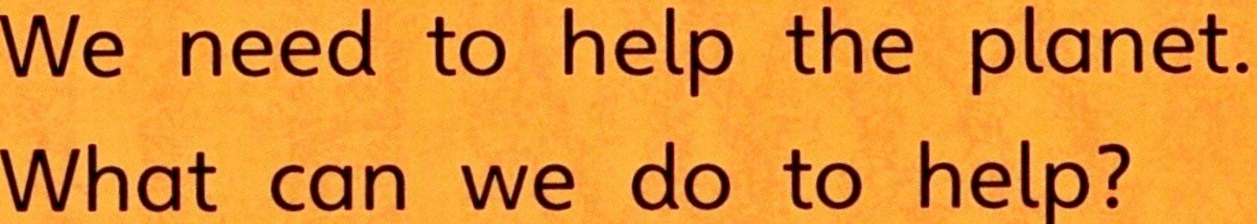

We need to help the planet.
What can we do to help?

Every year, each Australian family makes enough rubbish to fill a house!

I am with the Huli family. What are they doing to help the planet?

We can all **reduce, reuse** and **recycle** to help the planet!

Reduce: cut back on how much you use

Reuse: use things over and over

Recycle: make things into something different that can be used again

What are you doing to reduce what you use?

Use green bags, not plastic bags, to help the planet.

Every year, Australians use around 200 plastic bags each. That is bad!

What are you doing at home to reuse things?
I take a green bag when I go shopping.
I use jars and bottles over and over again.
PASTA SAUCE
JAM

Can you think of more things to reuse to help the planet?

What are you doing to recycle things?

There are lots more things we can recycle.

We can recycle food.

The food we do not use goes in here.
It will make **compost**.
We use it on the garden.

We can recycle things to make gifts for our friends.

We can all help the planet!
Remember to:

Glossary

compost soil made when grass, leaves and food scraps break down

energy a kind of power

rubbish things such as litter